INGENIOUS
GADGETS

INGENIOUS
GADGETS

Guess the obscure purpose of over 100 eccentric contraptions

MAURICE COLLINS
WITH IAN KEAREY

David and Charles

To my wife, Doreen, who has put up with
all my contraptions for 30 years.

A DAVID & CHARLES BOOK
David & Charles is a subsidiary of F+W (UK) Ltd.,
an F+W Publications Inc. company

First published in the UK in 2005

Distributed in North America
by F+W Publications, Inc.
4700 East Galbraith Road
Cincinnati, OH 45236
1-800-289-0963

A catalogue record for this book is available from the British Library.

ISBN 0 7153 2189 7 paperback

Printed in Singapore by KHL Printing Co Pte Ltd
for David & Charles
Brunel House Newton Abbot Devon

Commissioning Editor: Neil Baber
Editor: Jennifer Proverbs
Art Editor: Sue Cleave
Designers: Louise Prentice and Sarah Clark
Production Controller: Bev Richardson

Visit our website at www.davidandcharles.co.uk

David & Charles books are available from all good bookshops; alternatively you can
contact our Orderline on (0)1626 334555 or write to us at FREEPOST EX2 110,
David & Charles Direct, Newton Abbot, TQ12 4ZZ (no stamp required UK mainland).

Maurice Collins can be contacted at
mauricecollins@msn.com

Contents

Although I have been collecting for over thirty years, I still find it hard to define exactly what it is that I collect. The most fundamental definition is that the items in the collection were produced to solve everyday problems. To make a task simpler, quicker or easier.

It goes further. Is there a weird or absurd element in the invention? Does the task take actually more time to accomplish with the gadget than it would if you did it by hand or the old, established method? Or even better, did it succeed in performing its function better than inventions produced and sold in the 21st century to do the same thing?

The historical and economic influences that created the background to the innovation of the contraptions also has a bearing on how my collection has developed. The Great Exhibition in London in 1851 is my starting point, generating as it did a massive interest in new products, and began the promotion of products to a mass international market. It made the common man (the highest percentage of women to register a patent in the Victorian period was just under 3 per cent) aware that if a better solution could be found to any problem, it could be the source of fortune and success. At the same time as the Great Exhibition was in preparation, the British Government removed taxes on the publication of newspapers, and in 1855 the burdensome tax on advertising was also abolished. This gave the opportunity for new everyday products to be promoted and sold far more easily than before. The *Illustrated London News* for example, was launched in 1842 and within two years it had reached a circulation of 25,000. By 1863 it was well over 300,000, compare that to *The Times*, whose circulation at the time was only 70,000.

In the United States, which did not have the same tax restrictions as Great Britain, and where labour was scarce and expensive, the process of finding machines that would save time for the hard-pressed population created a burst of innovative products. Items such as the sewing machine, typewriter and the gramophone were all developed in the mid-to-late nineteenth century, and tens of thousands more patents were registered to attend to every conceivable situation in daily life.

The fact that patents were registered and the information is still obtainable gives a vast research resource to establish the use and background of the contraptions in my collection. The records go back to 1836 in the USA (an improved coat hanger was number 44,875, registered in 1864), and in England, Ireland and Wales from 1852.

So what are the items in the collection that give me the most pleasure? The ones that fit my criteria? Not always, take the asthma necklet (p192), sold in its thousands to unsuspecting sufferers; it looks good, plenty of customers in the promotional leaflet attest to its effectiveness, but as we all know, it's a con in the great tradition of quack medicine. The teapot, that when you press the lid delivers just one cup of tea (p144), is a favourite – it looks better and works more efficiently than many a modern tea or coffee pot. And I love the copper boot warmer that you can stand in with your boots frozen and it will thaw your footwear and your feet all at the same time (p86).

The items in the collection bear testament to those creative minds who spent time and money trying to solve everyday problems. If successful, the gadgets created employment, those who made and used them all paid tax, and the taxes brought the roads, public sanitation, social welfare and all the other services that society demands. So a big thank you to the mostly unknown inventors who made the world go round and have given me thirty years of pleasure trying to save their creative endeavours for the future.

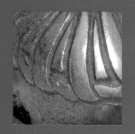

■ The Working Day

Nib extractor

This very unusual office desk item doubled
up as a paperweight and a nib extractor in
the pre-fountain pen days of the late 19th
century. Simply by placing the pen into
the small hole at the bottom of the glass
neck, pushing hard onto the nib and then
removing the pen shaft, the old nib would
be removed cleanly and a new one could
be inserted.

Attention getter

It may look like an old-fashioned rattle
for cheering a favourite football team or
perhaps waving at a parade or some other
major national event, but this Victorian
contraption was clamped to the desk
of a teacher, to calm down or gain the
attention of the rowdy pupils in the class.
Brilliant – and one or two teachers have
told us they'd like one nowadays.

Pen wiper

The manufacturer's advertisement gives a
pretty strong clue as to what this Victorian
ceramic device was used for. It was quite
simply for wiping the excess ink from your
pen nib and would happily have sat on
your desk as a reminder of where to get
some more when you'd wiped off the
last of it. No doubt given away free by
Blackwood and Cos. to good customers
and suppliers of their products.

Combination door lock

Using the power of clockwork, this simple
French gadget from around 1900 sounded
a high-pitched bell alarm if anyone
attempted to open the door to which it
was attached without knowing the pre-set
entry code. Unless the combination was
correctly entered, movement on the door
handle would cause the bell to swivel and
the alarm to go off.

'The pencil with a brain'

This was the claim by the manufacturers in the 1930s: a pencil that could do a range of fascinating calculations. The idea was that you could measure by rolling the pencil, with the distance indicated by the scale, and you could add, subtract, divide and multiply. Sadly, they failed to include Albert Einstein to explain the instructions.

Fuse remover

The fuses for shells used in World War
One were located in the head of the
shell case. Unexploded shells required
defusing by sappers; this well engineered
tool was designed to remove the offending
fuse easily enough, but it was always a
risky business.

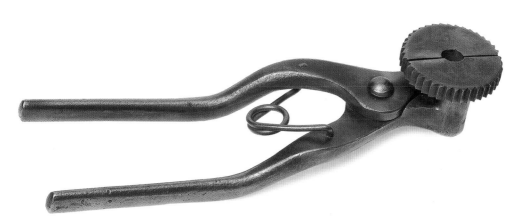

Ink purifier

We cannot fathom the thinking behind, or reason for this Edwardian patent, which is a glass moulded 'beehive' style receptacle with one pen dip hole. Inside are two small balls, made of what we know not. And why on earth would one want or need to purify ink – could it have been used for some religious or Masonic reason?

Horn trainer

At the time of writing, we have not
managed to get a definitive view on how
this gadget was used. It has even been
suggested that it is a birth control device
for sheep. Much more likely though is that
the weighted ends are placed over the
tips of an animal's horns and the straps
tightened to exert pressure in a particular
direction to make them grow evenly. The
same idea as a dental brace. After all, no
prize-winning cow or ram could afford to
have crooked horns.

Memorandum clock

John Davidson invented this contraption
in the 1890s to allow clients of the
professional classes to know when their
appointment was completed. The name
of the client was written in pencil on one
of the bone noteslips and when time was
up it would fall through the mechanism,
triggering an alarm that continued until the
noteslip was removed. Legend has it that
houses of ill repute (professionals who
charged by the hour) were also users of
this latest timing innovation.

Shop display arm

The consumer boom of the late 19th
century created purpose-built shopping
streets and the beginnings of the large
general stores we know today. Another
development was the invention of
mechanical moveable display arms to take
the many fashionable clothes demanded by
the Victorians. This American version was
also used in the wardrobes of the middle
classes to make storage and selection of
garments easier.

Collapsible megaphone

Could this have been used by coxes to shout rowing instructions at their oarsmen or was it used by the police to control crowds of demonstrators? Either way, the folding structure is a convenient way to carry the instrument for any control freak of the mid-1920s needing extra volume.

Page turner

This nicely made wooden whatsit of the
1920s advertises a varnish manufacturer
in East London. Such objects would have
been sent to the accounts departments to
allow the clerks to turn their large ledger
pages – and might just be a constant
reminder to pay their bills on time to this
particular generous supplier.

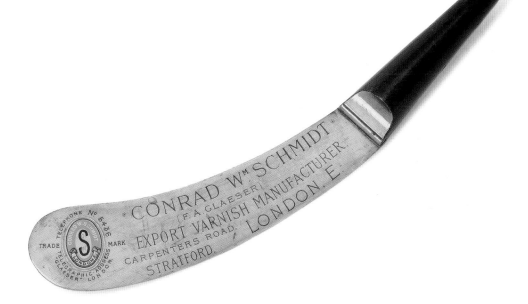

Market light

Until First World War government
restrictions put an end to nighttime
activities, most working-class districts in
London had small street markets that
would trade as late as 10 or 11 o'clock on
Saturday nights. What gas street lighting
there was did not shed much more than a
glow, so traders used lights that could be
attached to an upright on a stall. Thomas
Burke wrote evocatively of the 'sharp flare
and hiss of the naphtha lights' in London
street markets, reminding us that constant,
silent public lighting is a modern concept.

Pitch whistle

This clever whistle from the 1920s can be adjusted to sound at a variety of pitches. We think it was employed by brass band leaders to assist the players to tune their instruments, being able to provide different notes for all the antique plumbing systems and thus avoid undignified squabbles between the second euphonium and the trombones.

Envelope gluer/sealer

The 'Velopost' answered the prayers
of early 20th century direct marketing
companies in the USA: it automated the
gluing, flap-folding, wetting and sealing of
one or many envelopes, just by turning
the handle as fast as one could. As a direct
result doormats began to wear out much
more quickly under the weight of junk mail.

Explosion viewer

If you wanted to know how near the
shell blasts were to your trench in World
War One, this handy coloured-glass tool
allowed you to look at the explosions
without the glare affecting your eyes. The
problem was, of course, that you had to
put your head above the parapet…

Wrist fire siren

This watch-like contraption ensured that
anyone on guard duty or fire watch in the
1920s could immediately sound the alarm
by blowing the piercing whistle affixed
to their wrist. It could have been the
precursor to the mugging and rape alarm
contraptions that have become all the rage
today, but didn't spray the assailant with
anything more menacing than spittle!

Dice counter attraction

Any reason would do to keep the customers occupied once they were in American stores, and counter attractions came in many forms. In this 1940s example you simply had to press the lever and the dice spun – if you got a double six you could then get a discount on any item in the store.

Carton/box corner cutter

This simple but effective 1920s tool sliced
through the corner edges of any cardboard
carton to open it quickly and efficiently.
Such a cutter would be a boon for the
staff in today's supermarkets and retail
parks, so we offer it as an opportunity for
any young entrepreneur who might be
reading this book.

Pocket watch camera

The connection to the clock in the name
of this unusual mid-1920s camera refers to
the fact that it looks like a pocket watch,
not that it told the time. It claimed that the
owner was entitled to a '100% clear, sharp
and perfect picture' and that 'the film could
be developed in stores that did this type
of work'. You could always recognize those
places, as they were patronised by furtive
people with hats pulled down low and
coat collars turned up…

Pencil sharpener

The patents that were produced for the simple job of creating a point on a piece of lead ran into many thousands. This American example from the 1890s works via a complicated gear assembly that makes turning the handle easy and the point even sharper.

Chalk holder

The energy used to draw one chalk line
on the blackboard could, with this device,
draw five in one pass; chalks were placed
into the apertures at the end of the wire
prongs, and the holder was then ready for
use. It was designed initially, we believe,
for the teaching of music, (a musical stave
containing five parallel lines) but it would
certainly have made a particularly vicious
weapon to throw at any naughty lads at
the back of the class.

Sack tying machine

A simple but effective 1890s American
tool for tying sacks: quickly hook the
loose ends of the strings on the top of
the sack, then pull the centre bolt down
the Archimedean screw, which causes the
strings to plait and fasten immediately.

Hank/yarn winder

Made by Goodbrand and Co of
Manchester in the early 1900s, this
beautiful winder was used for testing
the strength of yarn. A hank of yarn
was selected from the latest delivery
and wound onto the winder. The bell
rang when a set length had been wound,
and the weight per length was then
calculated to check that the yarn was
of the right quality.

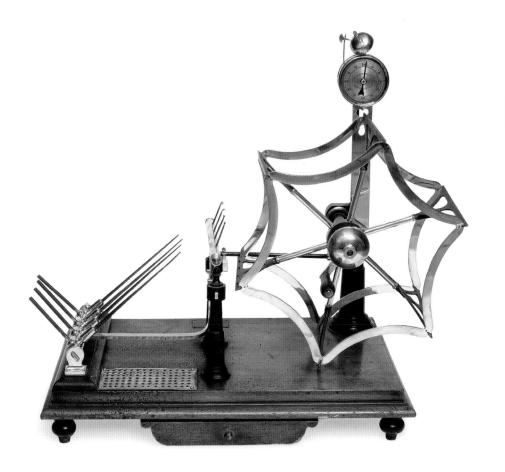

Inkmaker pen

No need for bottles of ink on manoeuvres;
make your writing fluid from water and
a concentrated-chemical battery already
in the pen, was the offer to American
soldiers in the field in World War Two. The
manufacturers claimed that the pen was
'streamlined, perfectly balanced, light as a
feather and leak proof', and so it probably
was, but the closely printed instruction
sheet is so complex that you'd revert
back to old-fangled pen and ink if you
needed to send that letter to your
sweetheart quickly.

Hat stretcher

Traditionally hats were made to measure. The introduction of mass production and fixed sizes prompted the invention of this device, which would exert pressure on a hat by the turning of the screw and gradually stretch your 'titfer' to the perfect size.

Seed sower

The promotional headline for this gadget
was that the 'Sowrite sows seeds at a
touch' and it seems to work extremely
well! You fill the bowl with seeds and,
holding and aiming with one hand, clip
the metal spring with a finger of your
other hand. Sure enough, the seeds neatly
emerge from the tube one by one.

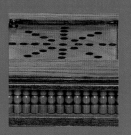

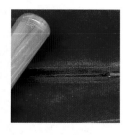   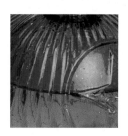

■ Domestic Economy

Replacement handle

So the handle on the teacup broke while it was being washed up. No problem – in the cutlery drawer resided the latest high-tech Victorian development: a tin handle replacement that fitted over the top of the rim and acted as your grip to carry on sipping your favourite broth.

Automatic cigarette extinguisher

In a few years the cigarette may well be a
thing of the past, but this innovation,
patented at the beginning of World War
Two, was the latest deterrent to fires
started by unattended lit cigs. As the
cigarette burns down its weight diminishes,
and the metal holder flips and squashes
the fiery tip to extinction. It seems rather a
shame to cover the delicate design with ash.

Tie press

This Sheffield-made deluxe tie press from
the late 1920s claims to press the most
creased tie as if it was ironed by hand: just
insert the centre board with the tie laid
around it into the wooden press, clamp for
a few minutes and hey presto! a tie fit for
the board meeting.

Cigar holder

Never have we seen even a photograph of a person using this particular Edwardian device; however, cigar holders were obviously popular at the time – Black Jack of Ballarat smoked his cigars through one in Conan Doyle's *The Boscombe Valley Mystery*, and Sherlock Holmes made his deductions via the presence of one in *The Resident Patient*.

Fur cleaner

Hardly PC today, this metal-pronged slicker
from the 1920s was wielded to keep
Mother's pride and joy, her long Russian
fitch coat and matching stole, looking sleek
and in the best of order. Now, we suppose,
you could use it to keep your Saluki in
prime condition and ready for the dog
show Crufts.

Spring-loaded candle holder

Keeping the light from a candle in one position as the wick burned down was a problem looking for an easy solution. By placing in the stem of the holder a spring that, as the wick burnt down, pushed the candle up, the Victorians could illuminate the same area until total burnout.

Tree/flagpole holder

For those without the space to have a tree or flagpole permanently positioned, the claws of this American heavy iron mechanical stand from the 1900s have a screw to tighten up on the base of the pole or trunk to hold it firmly in place over the Christmas jollities or, of course, for celebrations on Labor Day, Arbor Day, Groundhog Day and the Fourth of July.

Collar shaper

Edwardian office workers, unlike those of today, usually wore separate collars from their shirt. This handy little instrument allowed the housewife to ensure that the right 'curve' was placed into the collar while pressing it. We particularly wanted to include this gadget, to prove that 'Acme' brand goods are not just the preserve of Wile E. Coyote in his Sisyphean battle to entrap the Road Runner; how would he use this, we wonder?

Trouser crease holder

Front-and-back creases in trousers only came into fashion in the early 20th century – and inventors were quick to seize on the possibilities. This ingenious contraption keeps trousers, knickerbockers or plus fours in perfect condition. The holder has a screw that when turned, opens the crease holder to fit perfectly into the extremities of the trouser leg. When not in use, it folds down to fit into the purpose-built pouch.

Glass funnel cleaner

This American device was a boon to the
servant who was required to clean the
inside of the glass shades of oil lamps in
Victorian times, which always got covered
in soot from the burning of the wick. It
is inserted into the top of the glass and,
when pressed, the arms open up to create
the bulbous framework forming to the
shape of the glass; a cloth inserted into the
framework can then be turned to wipe
away the offending soot.

Boot and foot warmer

After you came in from the fields with
soaking wet boots, this device would be
waiting, the casing filled with boiling hot
water. You placed your booted feet into
the very large wells, and the heat very
quickly dried each boot and kept it to
the shape of your soon-warm foot. Made
of copper, this late-Victorian piece of
cleverness could have only been
afforded by aristocratic landowners
or wealthy farmers.

Top hat holder

Attached to the bar wall, this neat
American invention from the 1890s folds
away when not in use. The holder is
fixed in the entrance area, and pulling the
circular part down gives the well-heeled
visitor a place to put his top hat in a
safe and secure place while imbibing his
favourite tipple.

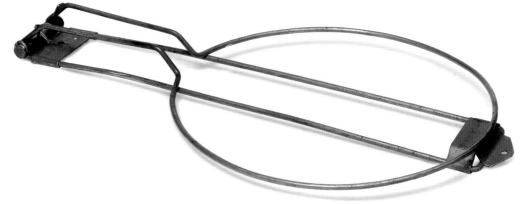

Cuff holder

This was called the 'wristband button and quick adjusting cuff holder', but, despite the manufacturer's claim that you could 'put cuffs off and on instantly and without raising the coat sleeve', it was most often used by card sharps to hide the ace up their sleeves at the poker tables of the Old West in the 1880s: 'Now, what would an honest man be doin' wearin' one of them things?'

Fire extinguisher grenade

The most common method of putting out
a fire in late Victorian and Edwardian times
was the fire grenade. This was filled with a
chemical extinguisher and thrown at the
flames; the glass container smashed on
contact and the specially prepared liquid
would hopefully extinguish the fire.

The Jadkin butter spreader

The need to butter bread for sandwiches at a rate of knots in a canteen or café, created a demand for this simple tool of about 1950, which would take the whole of a block of butter in one go, and then with one swipe completely cover a slice of bread. The hand on the handle and a finger pressing down the block of butter allowed a perfect film to be applied.

Magnifier

This simple magnifier from the 1920s, made to fit into a top pocket, is spring-loaded and returns automatically into its thin metal case. It's very handy for the intrepid beetle or fossil hunter or – dare we say it – gadget collector.

Shoe stretcher

This would have been used at the local
cobblers. It simply widened or lengthened
the shoe or boot by a twist of the
two side and back wheels; it was also
inadvertently a definitive way to test the
stength and resilience of 1930s boots
and shoes.

Fire blower

This beautifully engineered mechanical fire blower, used in stately homes of the late-Victorian period, stands about a metre (3ft) high and has lovely brass cogs. Turning the handle forces a stream of air in the direction of the embers of the fire, thus building up a roaring inferno.

Clockwork fly scarer

With a span of one metre (3ft), this
clockwork powered propeller revolved at
a very slow pace over the exposed food
on the Victorian dinner table. The large
spring, when fully wound, had the energy
to keep revolving for 15 minutes, just in
time to have all the diners sitting with their
knives and forks at the ready!

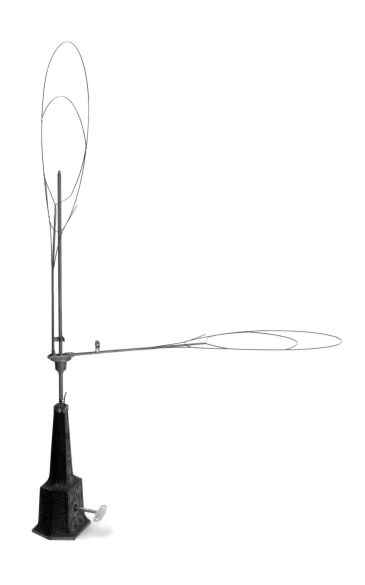

Fire bell

Called 'The Guardsman', this Canadian
bell from the 1920s has a clockwork
mechanism wound from the back. The
alarm then has to be set off by hand, as
a warning when a fire is seen. Although
the bell is loud, a verbal warning would
certainly be quicker and might do a better
job. The wee red flag is nice, though.

Card holder

This small gilded American contraption was used in the home to collect the calling cards of visitors, an unchanging element of etiquette in late-Victorian society for anyone with pretensions to gentility. If the person you were visiting was not available or, as appeared to be common, the lady of the house was acting demurely, you would leave your card by depressing the lever, and the hand held the card until the long-suffering maid retrieved it.

Bookmark

This most elegant little silver bookmark by Aspreys of Bond Street solved the dilemma of finding the present for the Edwardian man or woman who had everything. On affixing the device to the book jacket, the spring-held pointer fits onto the page being read, so that you always know where you are in the latest murder mystery.

Home dry cleaner

For those uninitiated in the art of dry
cleaning, the results are achieved by the
use of petrol or benzene. This natty device
from the 1920s, the Mutax, used a 'non-
flammable' spirit, thus doing away with the
danger of fire. The reservoir on the back of
the brush was filled with the spirit and the
clothes then brushed. It was claimed that
the spirit came down each bristle, giving a
great clean and, above all, saving money.

Bed cosy

This was made of a solid ceramic material that could be heated in the embers of a dying fire. Servants would then take the warmer and place it in the mid-Victorian master's bed to ensure that he would not have to rest in cold sheets; it was either that or the under-housemaid again.

Knot scissors

At last, scissors that 'save your nails, time, string and patience' and can also be used for every other practical purpose of ordinary scissors. Obviously knots were a problem in the early 20th century (I have a number of devices in my collection) – Baden-Powell and his Scouts had a lot to answer for.

Talking clock

It is believed that 300 of these brilliant but potentially irritating clocks were made by a German, B. Hillier. This one works by playing one of 48 tracks on a perforated celluloid film, one for each quarter of an hour to a maximum of 12 hours. When you think that 'talking films' didn't become properly marketable until the late 1920s ('You ain't seen nothin' yet, folks!'), this is pretty advanced technology for 1911.

Billiards cue sharpener

Dating from the early 20th century when
a mistimed attempt at a cannon in-off
could mess up the end of a cue, as well
as exposing one as a frightful duffer and
rabbit at billiards, this nifty guillotine tool
sharpens the damaged tip. Insert the front
end into the circular receptacle, press on
the finger hold, and the sharp steel blade
removes the damaged wood. A dash of
blue chalk, and back to the table you go.

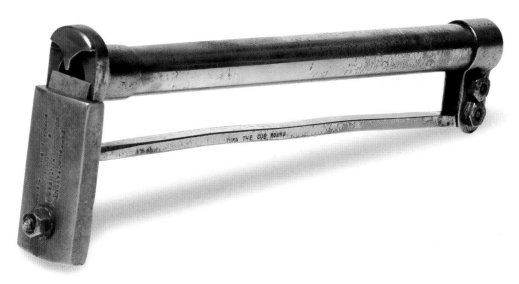

TURN THE CUB ROUND

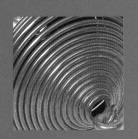

■ The Stuff of Life

Raisin stoner

Well, of course we all know this is a raisin
stoner from 1866, used for stoning raisins
(poor things) – but isn't it just so sinister
and beetle-like? We prefer to believe it
came to life at night and scuttled around
the rural kitchen, knocking into things
and scaring the living daylights out of
the family upstairs.

Electric kettle/teapot

This Czechoslovakian device from the
1930s should have been a runaway
success: a kettle that could also be used as
the teapot. It boiled the water, the whistle
announced when it was ready to receive
the tea, which was pre-prepared in the
strainer and was then lowered into the
boiling water to infuse and be ready to
pour. Perhaps it was the thought of having
to remove tannin as well as limescale from
the element that put buyers off.

Knife cleaner/sharpener

There are more patents for knife cleaners
than any other Victorian kitchen gadget,
and cover everything from small, simple
machines to more complicated dirt
removers, such as Mr Kent's fearsome
cleaner and sharpener, which stands 1.2m
(4ft) high and has the ability to clean six
(only six!) knives of any size in one go.
Place the powder in the machine, slot each
of the knives into the precise position, then
turn the handle. This all appears to take
more time than if you did the job by hand.

Crust scraper

This essential tool ensured that the master
of the house would not break his teeth
on a rogue hard crust. The rasp-like gadget
was used both in the home and in and
trade at the turn of the 20th century;
held by the wooden handle on the back,
one simply rubbed off unwanted hard
or burnt pieces of crust, like polishing
shoes with a shoebrush or using a sanding
block. Perhaps modern dental practice has
rendered it obsolete.

Flour mixer

Looking like a sculpture by Giacometti, this piece of 19th-century kitchenalia did the simple but necessary job of assisting the cook to mix flour for cakes or bread-making. By pressing and releasing the sides, the twirled wires expanded and returned, giving the ingredients a thorough seeing-to.

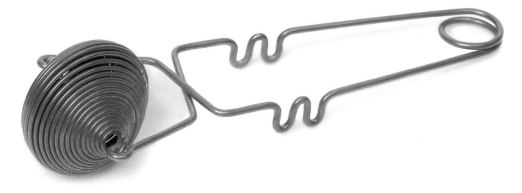

Miser's snuff box

Snuff-taking was a fairly expensive personal hobby, and good manners demanded that the Victorian gentleman offered a 'pinch' to friends and acquaintances. This little snuff container has a simple jagged brass pointer in between the finger holes – when taking your 'pinch' it ensures that only the smallest amount can be removed!

Ice cube cutter and scoop

This very unusual American gadget from
the late 19th century was used to make
ice cubes from the large solid blocks of
ice routinely delivered to pre-refrigerator
households. You placed boiling water in the
top of the melter, then positioned it on
top of an ice block until it formed the ice
into cubes; then you used the little scoop
to put the ice into the waiting mint julep.

Bottle lock

Those servants; you can't leave an open
bottle around without them taking a swig
when cleaning the cutlery – the servant
drunk on the house Madeira was a staple
of Victorian literature, theatre and *Punch*
cartoons. The simple mechanism of the
Burns lock of 1881 meant it could be
locked on the top of the bottle, and with
the key safely stowed in a pocket, nobody
could get at the drink when the master
wasn't around.

Olive stoner

Made of brass and wood this 'stoner' has
a simple but effective method of removing
the stones from the olive. Pressing the two
brass ears on the side allowed the olive
to be inserted, then releasing the ears
trapped the olive within the brass spout.
With the olive held in place, a press of the
plunger punctured the olive cleanly and
removed the offending pip.

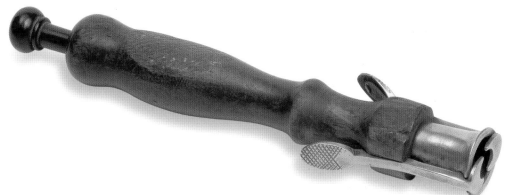

Butter safe

In a refrigerator-free world, keeping
perishable items like butter fresh was a
major concern. This butter safe claimed
that the cooling properties of the tin
drawer alone would keep the butter
cold; and the longer the butter was
kept in the safe, the colder and harder
it would become. It is difficult to imagine
how such a gadget would have stood up
to even moderately high temperatures
with any success.

Bottle opener and sealer

Metal crown corks should only be opened
with a tool of some description (and we
don't want to hear about your mate down
the pub who opens bottles with his teeth,
thank you). This clever American patent
from the 1950s had the added advantage
of being able to re-seal the top and keep
the gas in so you could drink the fizzy
liquid later.

One cup of tea dispenser teapot

The story behind this whatnot is that a
Mr Royle of Manchester patented a
ceramic and plated tin dispensing teapot
in 1886 to resolve the squabbles of his
children when pouring their tea: 'She's got
more than me!' Instead of tipping the pot
one draws up the lid and attached cylinder,
then holding a finger over a hole at its
tip and thus keeping it airtight pushes it
downwards back into the pot displacing,
and pushing out of the spout, exactly
one cup.

Bread cutter

Some contraptions have a real poignancy
about them. In the Depression era of the
1930s in the USA, families had to make
very little money go a long way, so this
simple but very effective 'Slice-a-Slice'
kitchen tool allowed an already thin slice
of bread to be cut even thinner, until you
could read the Want Ads through it. Those
on present-day diets please take note and
count your blessings.

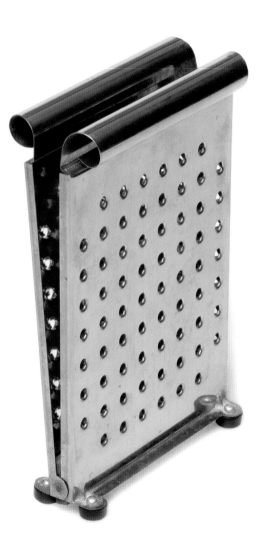

Lamp adaptor heater

This very simple but innovative thingy helped to adapt an oil lamp to the extra use of a coffee-making aid, or even to boil up water for a shave along the Chisholm Trail or in a variety of similarly uncivilized settings. The two lower prongs could be fitted into most lamp glass funnels, and the cup was placed on the stand above the flame. How quickly one could boil water from the heat of an oil lamp is not recorded but probably best to put your morning tea on the night before.

Automatic bottle lifter

There are no markings on this rather fearsome contraption from the beginning of the 20th century, but we believe that it was used to pick up different sized milk bottles from the doorstep of the rural American home – by pulling on the wire beneath the wooden handle the lower jaws clamp onto bottle-necks of various sizes. The reason, maybe, was to ensure that the lady of the house kept her hands hygienically clean.

Dough mixer

Before standard bread and Hovis came along, bought bread could contain all sorts of nasties, such as alum, chalk and lead, so making bread was a major time-consumer of the Victorian housewife. The ingredients were placed in the metal bucket-shaped container, and the geared handle ensured a good stir before the dough was placed in the oven and baked. The instructions are embossed on the lid, so you have to swing the handle fast to be able to read them.

Copper camping kettle

A lesson could be learnt by modern designers on how to maximize the heating of water by the simple idea of exposing more of the water to the heating source. In this outdoor tool from the 1920s the heat source was a fire of twigs and wood laid inside a cylindrical channel running through the kettle from top to bottom; the water surrounded the fire and was heated amazingly quickly. So effective is this practical gadget that a very similar design, the 'Kelly Kettle' is still available today.

Ice cracker

If you've ever wondered about how to crack ice for an Old-Fashioned, White Lady or Sidecar at your next suave cocktail party, this 1940s American gadget is the answer. A slight movement of the hand creates a vibrating motion in the handle; by placing it over the targeted ice and allowing the rhythmic movement of the tapper to continually hit the cube, the cracker causes the ice to shatter into a million pieces. Cheers!

Bird cooker

By winding up the clockwork mechanism
of this French whatchamacallit of the
1890s, the centre holder, containing the
bird to be barbecued over a fire, turns
very slowly, giving the opportunity for the
flesh to be well cooked and tender.

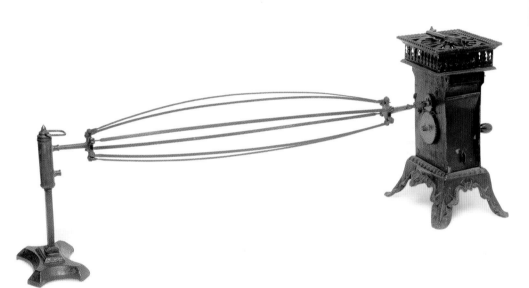

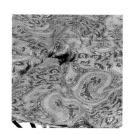

Out and About

Portable seat

The forerunner of today's fishing stools,
this Victorian contraption pulls apart and
fits into the small leather box. The inflatable
seat is supported by umbrella-like arms
which fold down neatly alongside the
central shaft. It was originally used, we
believe, by officers on military campaigns,
but it was just the ticket for fishermen,
picnickers and horse-racing buffs as well.

Ice-fishing rod

It may look as if it should be used to wind wool or to receive the *Grand Ole Opry* on station WSM, but in fact this is a rod that you lay over a hole in thick ice. The baited line goes into the water, where you leave it while you set up similar rods on the ice. The contraption is so arranged that any fish tugging on the line causes the red flag to wave, telling the fisherman that he's caught a live one.

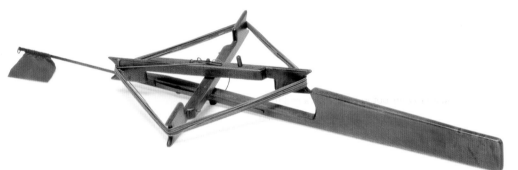

Bird Carrier

The 11 looped leather thongs with the brass buckles, all hanging from a wooden handle, allowed the bird game hunters to carry their partridge and pheasants' 'bag' easily and with the greatest of show for the benefit of their co-shooters. This was just one of the many innovations used in the British countryside to make life as easy as possible for the landed gentry.

Flutter fly

Toys don't usually make it into the
collection but this device is particularly
charming. Sold to keep children occupied
on car rides in the late 1920s, it works
by clockwork – when it is wound up the
wings flutter like a real insect – and it has
a sucker to stick it to the window of the
car. A far cry from Gameboys and iPods,
but a much more charming invention.

Tennis ball cleaner

Just the job for getting grassy stains off
Victorian tennis balls, the patent 'Kleenball'
lawn tennis ball cleaner, made of beautifully
turned wood in two separate halves, has
broom-like bristles meticulously fixed into
the inner edge of each half. By just placing
the soiled sphere inside the two parts and
turning in opposite directions any mud
or dirt could be removed efficiently and
quickly.

Whisky container

The drinking punter of the 1920s, not
wishing to have his vice exposed to
the world, could wear these imitation
binoculars around his neck while watching
the races. Thus he could take advantage
of having some of his favourite embalming
fluid ready at all times without adding to
the list of sins of commission in the eyes of
fellow race-goers.

Storm wipers

Before electrically operated windscreen
washers came into being, this natty
American invention ensured that your
windscreen would never be clouded over
with frost, ice or snow. Filled with a
specially formulated chemical, the Sleetex
wipers claimed to clear anything cold from
your windscreen, and boasted a universal
fixture process to fit most cars of the 1930s.

Sports glasses

When off to the races or at the ball game in 1940s America, these spectacles with binoculars attached gave you front row vision of your losing horse or fumbling footballer. You might walk into a lamppost on the way home, however, if you forgot to take them off for everyday sight.

Road skates

Bicycles had become a major form of
transport by the latter part of the 19th
century, and these skates, with their
high leather knee-securing bands, were
a logical development. Marketed, for
some reason, particularly at ladies, they
are beautifully made, with steel-spoked
wheels surrounded by solid rubber tyres
– a fascinating forerunner of today's
rollerblades.

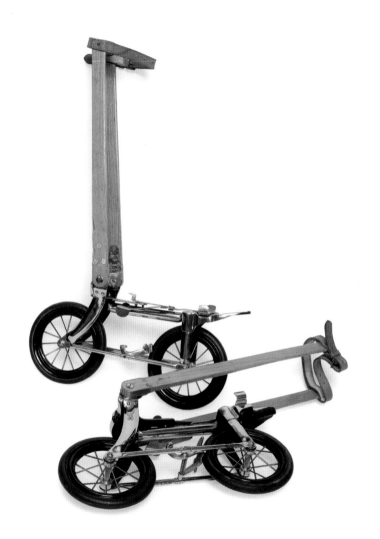

Tyre puncture repairer

There were no well co-ordinated road
breakdown organisations in the USA
or the UK at the beginning of the 20th
century, so when out motoring you had
to be totally self-sufficient. If you had
a puncture you attempted to mend it
yourself, using this dainty little instrument
of torture – unless of course the chauffeur
was driving, in which case you just lounged
around until you were roadworthy again.
It operates essentially as a clamp; a patch
of new rubber is glued to the tyre and
pressed into place by the spider-like fitting.
Pressure is exerted to keep the patch in
place by screwing the nut down.

Bicycle puncture detector

'A boon to cyclists' was the headline in the promotional material for this 1920s device. A simple and effective method of instantly locating and marking the minutest of punctures, without having to submerge the tyre in water. By placing powdered chalk on the metal mesh and gliding it slowly around the inner tube, any escaping air would blow a puff of chalk, instantly telling you where to apply the repair.

Spring-loaded glasses

Why on earth would you need to spring-load a dispenser for four drinking glasses? We don't know, but you can be sure we aren't going to put these 1920s American hoo-has in a picnic basket; they could put us right off our third bottle of fizz by the river… When packed away the glasses are held together under pressure; when the lid is released each glass pops out in turn, ready for use.

Rolling alarm clock

After winding this turn-of-the-century travel alarm up, you give it an 'inpulsion' (roll), which sets an internal pendulum working, enabling the alarm to go off at the pre-set time that you wish to be woken. Unbelievable the lengths the French will go to to get up on time!

Pattens

In the days before tarmac and proper
paving, bad weather conditions were
guaranteed to ruin shoes and stockings
– in Georgian London, paving stones that
tilted and shot mud up legs were known
as 'beaux traps'. These French pattens
from the 1860s are typical of what was
worn to counteract mud, snow and ice
in the country: the whole shoe is slipped
into the leather heel and toe, and an iron
hoop fixed to the wooden sole keeps the
wearer a few inches above the ground.

  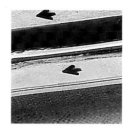 

■ Body and Soul

Asthma necklet

Mr Hillson, the maker, claimed that his
'scientifically constructed device in the
shape of a necklet which the sufferer
has simply to wear around their neck,
next to the skin' would enjoy perfect and
continued immunity from their former
trouble. The testimonials of the cure,
listed at the back of the 1910 instruction
pamphlet, attested to its success.
Unfortunately it is hard to see any
science at work here.

Nail buffer

Keeping their nails buffed to perfection
was an occupation enjoyed by many
a Victorian lady. This instrument was
obviously the deluxe version, as it provides
the opportunity both to change the buffing
material (velvet for weekdays and silk for
weekends) and produce different tensions
by use of the adjustable handles. Hooking
the thumb and little finger around the
provided grips pulls the buffer tight and
holds it securely for vigorous buffing.

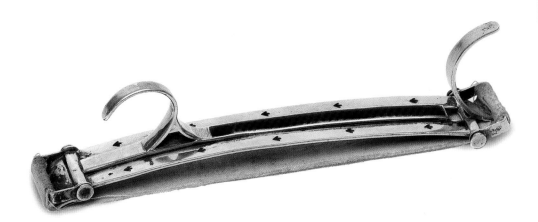

Comb strop

This 'Keep clean comb and hone strop'
in its original box is a very unusual
contraption of the Victorian period. Hung
on the wall in the 'ladies room' of the day,
it cleaned and sharpened up the comb's
prongs as the comb is drawn up and down
the threads. Why is hard to understand, but
perhaps the spread of hair lice hastened
the development of this novel patent.

Electric comb

A solution to hair loss for the man of the
1920s. The manufacturer claimed that the
use of this electrical appliance would make
hair grow where it didn't any more, and if
you already had a good head of hair, the
comb would prevent you losing it. The
electric comb and matching brush carried
on in production until the beginning of
World War Two, but didn't appear to
reduce the number of follicly challenged
gentlemen, if photographs are anything
to go by.

Automatic shaving brush

At last, something that would save time in
that early-morning rush to work: shaving
cream is placed in the handle, and by a
quick press of the plunger, it is inserted
into the hairs of the brush and you are
ready to start lathering. It's a great idea, but
the early 1940s was perhaps hardly a good
time to market German inventions outside
the domestic market.

Collapsible boot jack

Boot jacks dominated American mail-
order catalogues in the late Victorian
period, and this neat and simple example
collapses down to fit into a jacket pocket
or suitcase. Boots of the period were tight-
fitting and very difficult to remove – hence
the plethora of styles and designs for
instruments to shift them.

Myo-Onki Japanese wonder heater

This inventive 1950s hand-held ceramic heater was powered by two charcoal fuel bars which were inserted into the two holes at the top and would burn for about an hour. It claimed to give relief to all muscular aches and pains due to overwork and fatigue. No wonder the Japanese have a reputation for being punctual, fit and efficient!

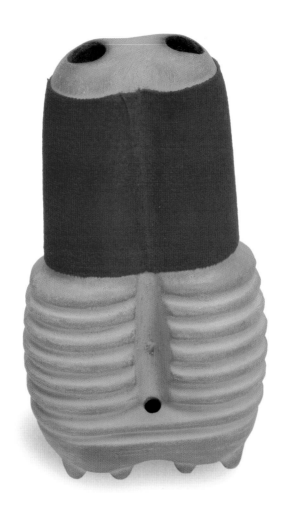

Sight restorer

The late 19th century 'Ideal Sight Restorer'
claimed that if the user persisted in
treatment, their vision would increase in
power day by day. All one had to do was
to apply the two eye cups against the
eyes, press the central air puffer and the
resulting massage would do the trick. The
instructions add that no excessive drinking
or eating and plenty of sleep should
occur at the same time as the treatment,
obviously hedging their curative bets!

Blackhead remover

American teenagers of the later 1940s
rushed to purchase this little gadget; in just
a few short minutes puberty could be at
an end, maturity would set in and, with
a little Brylcreem, courting could begin.
Vacuum-sucking out blackheads sounds a
bit like Tough Love compared to creams
and lotions, but nowadays it really doesn't
matter that much what you look like!

Perfuming brush

What a smart idea from the 1930s: fill the
detachable scent pad above the brush area
with your most seductive perfume – 'Allure
No. 2', no less – and while you tend to
your coiffure the brush automatically sends
the aroma into your curls.

Electro-massager

Zodiac, the manufacturers, claimed in 1909
that this gizmo was useful for treating
a variety of diseases and that it 'never
required re-charging and was always ready
for use'. Well, at least this latter bit is true:
you simply ran the machine up and down
over any affected parts and the dynamo
charger gave you a therapeutic shock.

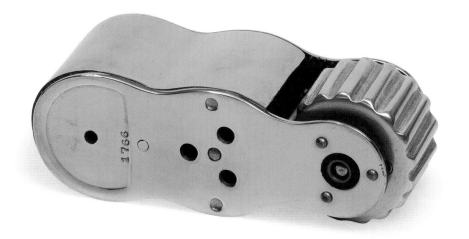

Trouser hooks

Hooray! No more 'builders bum'
syndrome for the fastidious Edwardians, as
these snazzy hooks ensure that your baggy
trousers will always be kept up near your
shirt or vest. But is this really the case? We
haven't been able to work out exactly how
they were used. A matching pair of hinged
steel hooks with a carrying case about
the size of a cigarette lighter, perhaps they
were made to replace errant fly buttons or
used as portable hangers. Their description
on the case as 'novelty' trouser hooks, only
adds to the mystery.

Wooden massager

A well-engineered quack medical item
from 1930s Japan with a very smooth
and invigorating action, this claimed to
remove any excess fat or relieve you of
any rheumatic pains. No doubt it did,
but we've tried it and the vibrations are
disconcerting, to say the least; turning the
handle causes the wooden pad to move
up and down very rapidly, giving the victim
a real pummelling.

Self-testing eye apparatus

In some ways, ophthalmic testing for magnifying reading glasses hasn't changed much. With this delicate but effective device, you place each eye to the optical glass at the front, and then move the tablet centre piece to the position which gives the clearest vision. You then read off your optical prescription, write away with that reading to the Self-test Optical Company of Chicago, and they will return the glasses that allow you to read proficiently (well, you could in 1928, but you might have to check they're still operating now).

Traction set

Dating from 1950s America, this particular
surgical appliance claimed to cure
backache and ricked necks. According to
the instructions, you hung one end from
a door frame, then suspended yourself
from your head and neck. For some
reason, the company doesn't appear to
be trading any more.

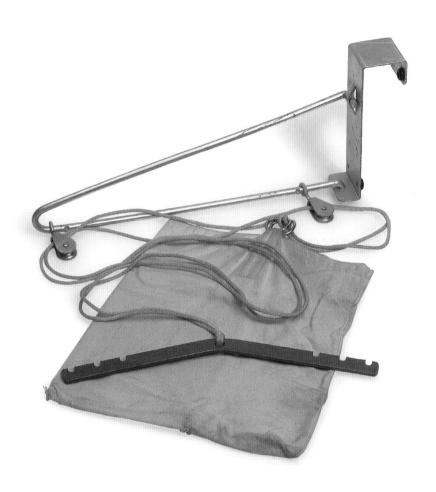

222

ACKNOWLEDGMENTS

Thanks to George Taylor for the photography in various locations across London, Sue Cleave and Neil Baber at David & Charles, and Ian Kearey.

Maurice Collins will be using the royalties from this book to assist in the opening of a museum dedicated to 'Weird Inventions, Gadgets and Everyday Technology' from the past, the WIDGET Museum. This will focus on all those forgotten everyday inventions that were designed to ease the burden of everyday life, and perhaps make the inventor both a name and financial success (which of course they rarely ever did).

For those who would like to know more about the Museum or the collection, Maurice can be contacted at mauricecollins@msn.com